SERIES TITLES

1945 TO THE COLD WAR
was created and produced by McRae Books Srl
via del Salviatino, 1
50016 Fiesole (Florence), Italy
info@mcraebooks.com
www.mcraebooks.com

Publishers: Anne McRae, Marco Nardi
Art Director: Marco Nardi
Series Editor: Anne McRae
Author: Neil Morris
Layouts: Nick Leggett, Starry Dog Books Ltd
Title Editor: Vicky Egan
Project Editor: Loredana Agosta
Research: Vicky Egan
Repro: Litocolor, Florence

Main illustrations: Francesca D'Ottavi: 28-29, 35, 42-43;
MM Comunicazione (Manuela Cappon, Monica Favilli,
Gianni Sbragi, Cecilia Scutti) pp. 30-31; Paola Ravaglia:
3, 26-27, 40; Studio Stalio (Alessandro Cantucci,
Fabiano Fabbrucci, Margherita Salvadori): 16-17.

Other illustrations: Lorenzo Cecchi, Matteo Chesi,
Giampiero Faleschini, MM Comunicazione
(Manuela Cappon, Monica Favilli, Gianni Sbragi,
Cecilia Scutti), Paola Ravaglia, Studio Stalio (Alessandro
Cantucci, Fabiano Fabbrucci, Margherita Salvadori)

Maps: Julian Baker, Paola Baldanzi

Photos: THE ART ARCHIVE: 8-9b; ©Abram Games
by SIAE 2009 / The Art Archive / Eileen Tweedy: 18al;
The Art Archive / Gianni Dagli Orti: 22br; The Art
Archive / Imperial War Museum: 9al; The Art Archive /
National Archives Washington, DC 10c, 14ar, 42al.
THE BRIDGEMAN ART LIBRARY: 17br, 18ac, 20b, 36bl.
©Dedda71: 39cr. THE IMAGE WORKS, INC.: Bill
Bachmann / The Image Works: 34ar; Charles Gatewood
/ The Image Works: 45ar; Françoise de Mulder / Roger-
Viollet / The Image works: 40-41a; DoD / Roger-Viollet
/ The Image works: 38-39b; Mark Godfrey / The Image
works: 29al; Andrew Lichtenstein / The Image Works:
39cl; Manchester Daily Express / SSPL / The Image
Works: 6bl, 23b, 45cl; Mary Evans Picture Library /
Eddie Bairstow / The Image works: 38bl; Mary Evans
Picture Library / Roger Mayne / The Image works: 19c;
John Nordell / The Image Works: 25al, 43br; RIA /
Topham / The Image Works: 37cr, 40ar; Science
Museum / SSPL / The Image Works: 10-11b; SV-
Bilderdienst / The Image Works: 6-7cb, 32cbl, 36-37b;
Topham / The Image Works: 12bl, 18-19c, 19ar, 22cl,
25b, 26cl, 28cl, 38c; 44-45c; US National Archives /
Roger-Viollet / The Image works: 6al, 14-15b, 22ar.
ISTOCKPHOTO: ©Edward Hor / Istockphoto: 45al;
©Robert Reid / Istockphoto: 35ar; ©Wojciech
Zwierzynski / Istockphoto: 13ac; ©Anna Yu /
Istockphoto: 39al. THE KOBAL COLLECTION: Columbia /
Goldcrest / The Kobal Collection: 12-13b.
MARCO LANZA (FLORENCE): 17al. NASA: 32br, 33, 33al,
34cl. COURTESY RONALD REAGAN LIBRARY: 23ar, 38ar.

Consultant: Professor William Scott Lucas, Professor
of American Studies, University of Birmingham, UK

LIBRARY OF CONGRESS CATALOGING-IN-PUBLICATION DATA

1945 to the Cold War
  ISBN 9788860981844

2009923552

Printed and bound in Malaysia.

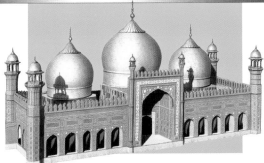

1945 to the Cold War

Neil Morris

Consultant: Professor William Scott Lucas
Professor of American Studies, University of Birmingham, UK

Contents

TIMELINE

	1945	1951	1957	1963
THE UNITED STATES	Launch of the Marshall Plan 1947.		The USA sets off its first H-bomb on October 31, 1952 on Enewtak, an atoll in the Pacific.	The Cuban missile crisis. / August 1963, Martin Luther King gives his "I have a dream" speech. In November, President John F. Kennedy is assassinated. John Glenn is the first US astronaut to orbit Earth.
THE SOVIET UNION	The Yalta Conference is held in the Crimea, Soviet Union.		1957 sees the launch of Sputnik 1 and Sputnik 2—the first artificial satellites in space.	A "hot line" (direct communications link) is set up between the leaders of the US and USSR, to deal with international crises.
EUROPE	The Potsdam Conference is held near Berlin, Germany.	Elizabeth II is crowned Queen of England, 2 June 1953.	Charles de Gaulle becomes president of France, 1958.	The Berlin Wall is built, 1961. The EEC introduces a Common Agricultural Policy (1962), which affects farming practice throughout Europe.
ASIA		The Korean War (1950–53).	In China, the Great Leap Forward is introduced (1958) to increase industrial output, but fails.	Start of the Vietnam War (1959–75). / Mao launches the Cultural Revolution in China, 1966.
THE MIDDLE EAST	The modern state of Israel is founded, 1948.		Egypt nationalizes the Suez Canal in 1956, leading to the Suez War.	US troops enter Lebanon to restore order.
AFRICA			1954–62, the Algerian war of independence from France. In 1956 Sudan, Tunisia, and Morocco become independent.	1960 sees 17 African countries gain independence. More follow over the next few years.
CENTRAL AND SOUTH AMERICA	Juan Perón becomes president of Argentina, 1946.		In 1952, Eva Perón, wife of the Argentine president and champion of the working classes, dies aged 33.	Brasilia replaces Rio de Janeiro as capital of Brazil in 1960.

Introduction

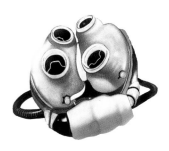

After the end of the Second World War, a political divide quickly opened up between the Allied victors. Distrust and suspicion led to hostility between the United States and the Soviet Union, along with their respective allies. This came to be known as the Cold War, which led to involvement in various conflicts around the world but never to direct military confrontation. The fear of nuclear war was felt everywhere and increased during periods of heightened tension. The situation altered during the 1980s, when reforms and political uprisings led to great changes in the Eastern bloc. This book tells the story of the Cold War from its beginnings in 1945 to the break-up of the Soviet Union in 1991. It covers events around the world, including wars in Korea and Vietnam, changes in newly independent India and Mao's China, struggles in Africa and the Third World, and the development of peace and human rights movements.

Monument to the Vietnamese Communist leader Ho Chi Minh (1890–1969), who became president of North Vietnam.

The first artificial heart was implanted by American surgeon William DeVries in 1982. It was made of plastic and aluminium.

1969

The Apollo 11 mission lands the first men on the Moon.

The Watergate scandal of 1972 leads to the resignation of President Nixon in 1974.

The Sino-Soviet split reaches a peak. There are armed border clashes between China and the USSR.

Start of the Troubles in Northern Ireland.

Death of Ho Chi Minh, president of North Vietnam.

1975

A US Apollo spacecraft docks with a Soviet Soyuz craft in space (1975).

Cold War tensions begin to ease.

1976, North and South Vietnam unify into a single nation.

October 1973, the Yom Kippur War is fought between Israel and a coalition of Arab states led by Egypt and Syria.

In Uganda, a military coup brings Idi Amin to power in 1971. His brutal regime lasts for 8 years.

Civil war in Nicaragua, 1976–79.

1981

Ronald Reagan is 40th President of the USA (1981–89).

In December 1979, Soviet troops invade Afghanistan. Fighting continues for 9 years.

The Chernobyl nuclear disaster, 1986.

Margaret Thatcher is first female Prime Minister of the United Kingdom (1979–90).

1978, Vietnamese forces invade Cambodia, driving out Pol Pot and the Khmer Rouge.

The first Intifada—a popular uprising of Palestinian refugees living in Israel—starts in 1987.

Drought causes terrible famines in Ethiopia in 1984–85, killing about 1 million people.

The International Court of Justice decides that the US acted illegally in aiding the Contras in Nicaragua (1986).

1987

1993

In the Gulf War (1990–91), the US leads a coalition force that forces Iraq to leave Kuwait.

In December 1991, Mikhail Gorbachev resigns as Soviet president and the Soviet Union breaks up.

1989, the Berlin Wall is knocked down.

The Vietnamese leave Cambodia after an 11-year occupation.

Tiananmen Square protest and massacre in China (1989).

The Gulf War, 1990–91.

Augusto Pinochet steps down as president of Chile, 1990.

Communists Versus Non-Communists

The post-war creation of two Korean states—the Communist Democratic People's Republic in the north and the non-Communist Republic of Korea in the south—led to a real "hot" war by 1950. The Korean War (see page 24) included the first use of United Nations troops in battle, on the side of the South Koreans.

Korean children walk beside an American M-26 tank in 1951.

World Divisions

During the Cold War the world was divided by political aims and ideologies. The United States and its allies viewed Communism as a threat to democracy. They accused the Soviet Union of trying to spread Communism throughout the world. The Soviets, on the other hand, accused their opponents of practising imperialism and stopping popular revolution. The rift widened until the downfall of the Soviet system led to a form of unity between East and West.

East German police talk to West Berliners across the wall that was put up by the Soviet-backed Democratic Republic in 1961 (see page 16).

Boom Years

The economic difficulties of the immediate post-war period in the United States were followed by growth and prosperity in the 1950s. The boom, which created a predominantly affluent American society, spread to western Europe. Later it also transformed Japan and the region of Southeast Asia (see pages 42–43), while the Soviet Union concentrated on rebuilding heavy industry.

By the late 1950s, British grocers, like other shopkeepers, had many more goods to offer their customers.

Connecting People

During the 1950s, the growth of television led to the world becoming a smaller place to many people. In the 1960s, the launch of communications satellites gave people instant access to global events. America's Telstar satellite transmitted the first live transatlantic television signals in 1962. This led to enormous progress in telecommunications, a fashionable term in the 1970s, though people in the Soviet bloc were not allowed the same access.

Divided World

During the Cold War period the world split into three groups. The first two worlds were those directly involved in the Cold War: the United States, western European industrial nations and Japan on the one side; the Soviet Union and other Communist nations, especially in eastern Europe, on the other. The so-called Third World was made up of developing countries in Africa, Asia and Latin America.

A TV guide from the 1950s. The television set quickly became the focal point of many families' lives.

Into the Computer Age

Computers of the 1950s were huge, complicated machines. They were gradually introduced into large businesses, mainly for accounting purposes, but were of little interest to smaller companies or ordinary people until the 1970s. Then the introduction of smaller, more user-friendly personal computers (PCs) led to the launch of a revolution in information technology (IT). Word processing, simple data operation and games programs made computers much more desirable by the beginning of the 1990s.

By the 1980s, personal computers were being used in schools and by many young people at home.

The three leaders at Yalta: Winston Churchill (UK), Franklin D. Roosevelt (USA) and Joseph Stalin (USSR).

The Post-War World

The end of the Second World War led to the occupation of Germany by the four major powers. German war criminals were tried, and as reconstruction began, the United States made plans to help economic recovery throughout Europe. At the same time, the Soviet Union helped Communist governments take power in Eastern European countries such as Czechoslovakia, Hungary, and Poland. The new United Nations organization was formed to address the kind of tensions that were already developing.

Decisive Meetings

The post-war occupation of Germany was discussed by the "Big Three" nations at the Yalta and Potsdam conferences in 1945. By the end of the second conference, the nations were led by British Prime Minister Clement Attlee, US President Harry S. Truman, and Soviet Premier Joseph Stalin. By this time the Soviet Union had helped establish Communist governments in the Eastern European countries that it had liberated from German rule. The other two nations resented and criticized this.

OCCUPIED GERMANY

Controlled Zones

After the war, Germany was divided into four zones controlled by Britain, France, the Soviet Union and the United States. The Soviet Union also controlled East Prussia, and territory east of the Soviet zone came under Polish administration. Berlin, in the Soviet zone, was divided into four sectors.

- British zone
- American zone
- Soviet zone
- French zone
- Polish admin.
- Soviet admin.

Map labels: DENMARK, NETHERLANDS, EAST PRUSSIA, HAMBURG, BREMEN, HANNOVER, BERLIN, WARSAW, DÜSSELDORF, LEIPZIG, POLAND, BONN, FRANKFURT, PRAGUE, CZECHOSLOVAKIA, STUTTGART, FRANCE, MUNICH, VIENNA, AUSTRIA, HUNGARY, SWITZERLAND

Legacy of Destruction

The war had caused devastating destruction throughout Europe. Cities across the continent lay in ruins. The Polish capital of Warsaw, which had been captured by the Germans at the very beginning of the war, was almost completely destroyed. The German capital of Berlin was left in ruins by Allied bombing raids and a land battle at the end of the war. Children of many nationalities were orphaned, and surviving soldiers returned from battle to search in vain for their homes and families.

The Marshall Plan

In 1947, US Secretary of State George C. Marshall proposed a European Recovery Program, agreed by Congress the following year. The Marshall Plan invited European nations to list their requirements for economic recovery, to be met by financial grants, loans, food and machinery. Seventeen countries formed the Organization for European Economic Cooperation, but the Soviet Union stayed out. In the first two years nearly $12 million were distributed, mainly to Britain, France, Italy and West Germany.

A German poster urges free passage for the Marshall Plan.

A woman wheels her few belongings through a Berlin street in 1946. About a third of the city was completely destroyed.

United Nations

The former League of Nations, which had not operated during the war, was replaced in 1945 by a new United Nations organization. The UN Charter created a Security Council of five permanent members— China, France, the Soviet Union, the UK and the USA—and ten non-permanent members elected to two-year terms by a General Assembly. Importantly, the Security Council was given the power to ask UN members to provide military peacekeeping forces to settle international disputes.

The UN flag and an Indian member of a UN peacekeeping force.

In this painting, the Nuremberg defendants are surrounded by the destruction they caused.

Nuremberg Trials

From November 1945, leading Nazis were tried at Nuremberg for war crimes and crimes against humanity. There were eight judges, two each from the powers occupying Germany. Twelve military leaders were sentenced to death by hanging, and others received long prison sentences. Hitler, Goebbels, Goering, and Himmler had committed suicide. Later, Nazi party officials and others were tried.

THE POST-WAR WORLD

1945

Feb 4–11: The Yalta Conference is held in the Crimea, Soviet Union.
April 12: US President Franklin D. Roosevelt dies.
Jun 26: All 50 nations present at a conference in San Francisco vote to accept the UN Charter.
Jul 17–Aug 2: The Potsdam Conference is held just outside Berlin, Germany.
Oct 24: The UN Charter is ratified at a meeting in London (and the date becomes the annual United Nations Day).

1946

Jan 3: William Joyce (known as Lord Haw Haw), who broadcast on behalf of Nazi Germany, is hanged in Britain for treason.
April: Tokyo War Crimes Trial begins in Japan.
October: End of the first trial conducted by the International Military Tribunal at Nuremberg.

1947

March: President Truman declares that the US will help any nation resist Communist aggression (the Truman Doctrine).
June: The US proposes to provide aid to Europe via the European Recovery Program. George C. Marshall says the policy is directed at "hunger, poverty, desperation and chaos."

Start of the Cold War

The United States and the Soviet Union were the world's two major powers after World War II, in which they had been allies. Yet as the Soviets expanded their Communist influence throughout Eastern Europe, they quickly made enemies of the Americans in what became known as the Cold War. Though this never turned into open warfare, there was always the threat of nuclear devastation as the arms race escalated.

The US/UK Berlin airlift of 1948–49 prevented the city being cut off during a Soviet blockade (see Timeline, left).

Red Scare Period

From 1950 to 1954, Republican Senator Joseph McCarthy ruthlessly pursued his claims that Communist spies and sympathizers had found their way into all parts of American life. During this age of so-called McCarthyism, many academics, artists, entertainers, and journalists came under suspicion and were investigated by the Un-American Activities Committee. Many employees were required to take oaths of loyalty to the US government in order to keep their jobs.

Senator McCarthy waves his list of supposed Communist sympathizers in the State Department in 1950. The US Army Information Division poster (above) appeared six years later.

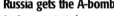

By the 1950s, some people were investing in anti-radiation suits.

Iron Curtain

In 1946 the former British war leader Winston Churchill said in a speech that a shadow had fallen across the Allied victory. "From Stettin in the Baltic to Trieste in the Adriatic, an iron curtain has descended across the Continent," Churchill went on. He was referring to the militarized border between the newly developed Communist bloc and western Europe. The Iron Curtain prevented free movement of people and ideas.

Russia gets the A-bomb

In August 1949, four years after the US dropped the world's first atomic bombs on the Japanese cities of Hiroshima and Nagasaki, the Soviet Union exploded its own atomic bomb. It was a test explosion in Kazakhstan of a plutonium bomb called First Lightning, which was similar to the Nagasaki device. The successful Soviet test came much earlier than US scientists and politicians expected, and in many people's minds it raised for the first time the horrendous possibility of nuclear war.

Scientists watched the nuclear tests from a distance with only sunglasses for protection.

Nuclear Arms Race

The first Soviet test explosion triggered a nuclear arms race between the US and its allies and the Soviet bloc. The race included both the number of bombs and their individual power. In 1955, three years after the US, the USSR set off its own H-bomb.

NUCLEAR WEAPONS BUILD-UP		1950	1960	1989
US	Warheads	350	18,700	22,500
	Megatons of TNT	77	19,000	11,000
USSR	Warheads	5	1,700	32,000
	Megatons of TNT	0,1	500	4,500

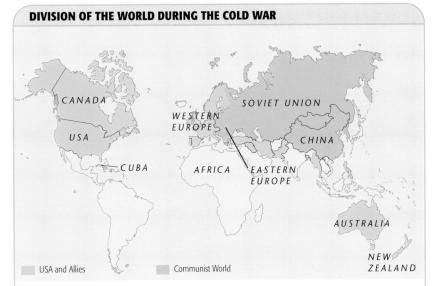

Joseph Stalin (1879–1953), the Soviet dictator who led his country into the Cold War.

Internal Hostility

As the Cold War progressed, there were internal tensions within the Soviet Union and the Communist bloc. In 1952 several important Jewish Czech politicians were charged with being traitors to the USSR and hanged. Then Stalin investigated an alleged conspiracy by Jewish doctors to poison the Soviet leadership. After Stalin died, in March 1953, Soviet repression and the Cold War eased slightly.

This was the mushroom-shaped cloud produced by the first American H- (for hydrogen) bomb, tested at Enewetak atoll in the South Pacific in 1952. It was hundreds of times more powerful and destructive than earlier A-bombs.

DIVISION OF THE WORLD DURING THE COLD WAR

CANADA

USA

CUBA

WESTERN EUROPE

AFRICA

EASTERN EUROPE

SOVIET UNION

CHINA

AUSTRALIA

NEW ZEALAND

■ USA and Allies   ■ Communist World

East versus West

The Soviet Union and China dominated the Communist world during the Cold War. Their allies were the Eastern European states, which were satellites of the USSR, and Cuba, placed conveniently close to the USA. Australia, New Zealand, Canada, and the Western European NATO countries were all on the American, non-Communist side.

Independence for India

The Indian subcontinent underwent huge changes during this period. The independence movement gathered pace swiftly at the end of the Second World War. The ruling British handed over power and by 1947 India was independent, along with a new Muslim state of Pakistan. Religious differences and mass migrations between the partitioned states led to violence. There was further unrest between Hindus and Sikhs, and between Muslims until the creation of Bangladesh.

Partition

Pakistan became independent on 14 August 1947, and India followed the next day. Pakistan (meaning "land of the pure" in Urdu) was itself divided, with India between West and East Pakistan. More than 10 million people became refugees, as Muslims fled to Pakistan and Hindus and Sikhs to India. Hindu–Muslim riots cost about half a million lives during this partition period.

Muslim refugees pack a train as it leaves Delhi for their new homeland in 1947. Others travelled on bullock carts, and millions went on foot.

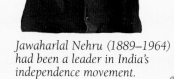

Charismatic Leaders

Jawaharlal Nehru was Prime Minister of India from independence until his death in 1964. Two years later, Nehru's daughter Indira Gandhi came to power. In Pakistan, the first leader was Muhammad Jinnah. In 1988 Benazir Bhutto became the first female leader of a Muslim country.

Indira Gandhi (1917–84) was Indian leader for a total of 16 years.

Jawaharlal Nehru (1889–1964) had been a leader in India's independence movement.

The 17th-century Badshahi mosque in Lahore, which became capital of the Pakistani province of West Punjab in 1947.

The Muslim–Hindu Divide

The president of the Muslim League, Muhammad Ali Jinnah, had been demanding a self-governing Muslim homeland since 1940. By 1946 the League feared that an independent India would be dominated by the Indian National Congress and the Hindu majority. Jinnah called for a Day of Direct Action, in which Muslims demonstrated for a separate state. This was followed by violent riots between Muslims and Hindus in Calcutta and other Indian cities.

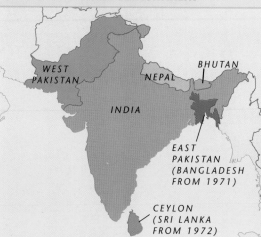

THE NEW SUBCONTINENT

WEST PAKISTAN

BHUTAN

NEPAL

INDIA

EAST PAKISTAN (BANGLADESH FROM 1971)

CEYLON (SRI LANKA FROM 1972)

Pakistan and Bangladesh

The people of West Pakistan and East Pakistan (later Bangladesh) spoke different languages (officially Urdu and Bengali respectively) and had different cultures. Though the eastern population was higher, the West contained the capital (Karachi and then Islamabad) and controlled the economy. Tensions grew and civil war broke out in 1971, killing thousands and making millions more refugees. Bangladesh (the "Bengal nation") became independent later that year.

Benazir Bhutto (1953–2007), daughter of the founder of the Pakistan People's Party, herself led the Party.

The Golden Temple in Amritsar, center of the Sikh faith.

Celebrating crowds wave the flag of the Indian National Congress, which became the national flag of India. The orange stripe stood for Hindus, the green for Muslims, with a "wheel of law" at the center.

Attack on the Golden Temple

In the early 1980s, an extreme group of Sikhs increased their demands for an independent state of Punjab, in northwest India. Prime Minister Indira Gandhi saw this as a threat to Indian unity and ordered troops to attack armed Sikhs in their holiest temple, the Golden Temple in Amritsar. Many hundreds of Sikhs were killed. Five months later, Mrs Gandhi was assassinated by two Sikh members of her bodyguard. Her son Rajiv succeeded her as prime minister.

INDEPENDENCE FOR INDIA

1948
Mohandas Gandhi is assassinated. Burma and Ceylon gain independence.

1959
The capital of Pakistan moves from Karachi to Islamabad.

1962
India loses a border war with China.

1965
India and Pakistan fight over Kashmir.

1966
The Punjab is divided into a Sikh-majority state of the same name, and Hindu-majority Haryana and Himachal Pradesh.

1970
A cyclone and tsunami strike East Pakistan, killing about 266,000 people.

1971
India signs a treaty of friendship with the Soviet Union.

1974
India explodes its first nuclear bomb in an underground test.

1984
Poisonous gas from a pesticide plant in Bhopal (in central India) kills more than 2,800 people.

1991
Indian Prime Minister Rajiv Gandhi (son of Indira Gandhi) is assassinated.

The Foundation of Israel

Since the late 19th century, Zionists had sought to establish a Jewish homeland and nation in Palestine. After the Second World War, many Jewish survivors of the Nazi Holocaust migrated to Palestine. In 1947 the United Nations proposed that a Jewish nation should exist alongside an Arab state. In 1948 the modern state of Israel was founded. This caused the first of the Arab-Israeli conflicts that were to go on until the present day.

This man was released from Buchenwald concentration camp when it was liberated in 1945.

The new Israeli flag showed the Star of David and the colors of the Jewish prayer shawl.

A New Jewish State

In 1947 the UN recommended creating separate Jewish and Arab states in Palestine, but Arab leaders refused to accept this. Fighting broke out and Zionist forces secured control of their intended lands and captured positions in Arab areas. On 14 May, 1948, the new state of Israel was proclaimed under the leadership of David Ben-Gurion, and was immediately recognized by the United States and the Soviet Union. The next day, the British ended their mandate in Palestine.

The Holocaust

The Nazi program of mass murder, which killed six million Jewish people, led to greater demands for a separate Jewish state after the war. The British had supported this at the end of the First World War, yet they still limited Jewish immigration to Palestine while it was under their control. Other countries also resisted immigration, increasing the despair of Holocaust survivors who did not wish to return to their pre-war homes, now under Communist rule.

Occupied Territories

The lands gained by Israel throughout the Arab-Israeli conflict are usually referred to as "occupied territories." They include the Golan Heights, Sinai Peninsula (1973–79), West Bank and Gaza Strip. Throughout the period the possession of these territories was disputed, since they were originally part of the Arab state proposed by the UN.

State of Israel as proclaimed 1948

Subsequent acquisitions

Temporary acquisitions

ISRAEL 1948–82

CYPRUS

South-Central Lebanon 1982 only

South Lebanon, occupied 1982

LEBANON

Kuneitra Strip 1967, returned to Syria 1974

SYRIA

JERUSALEM

Gaza Strip, occupied 1967

ISRAEL

Golan Heights, occupied 1967

Suez Perimeter 1973 only

West Bank, occupied 1967

East Jerusalem, annexed 1967

Sinai 1967, returned to Egypt 1982

Gulf of Suez

Gulf of Aqaba

EGYPT

Red Sea

Occupied territories

War in Palestine

In 1948, Arab forces from surrounding countries immediately attacked the new state of Israel. The forces came mainly from Egypt, Syria, Lebanon, Iraq and Transjordan. By early 1949, the Israelis had gained about half the land intended for the new Arab state of Palestine. Egypt and Jordan controlled the rest of Palestine. The UN intervened and by mid-1949 Israel had agreed an armistice with its neighbors, who would not sign peace treaties because they did not officially recognize Israel.

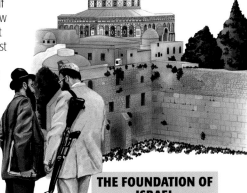

In times of conflict, some Israelis carried weapons as they went about their daily business.

The PLO

The Fatah organization was founded in 1958 by Yasser Arafat to fight for an Arab Palestinian state. Six years later, Fatah joined other groups to form the Palestine Liberation Organization (PLO). Arafat persuaded the UN to recognize the PLO as the official representative of Palestinian Arabs. In 1988, the PLO recognized Israel's right to exist alongside a Palestinian state in Gaza and the West Bank, both of which Israel occupied.

Originally a Palestinian guerrilla soldier, Yasser Arafat (1929–2004) eventually received the Nobel Peace Prize.

Invasion of Sinai

After Egypt closed the Suez Canal and the entrance to the Gulf of Aqaba to Israeli shipping, relations between Israel and Egypt worsened. In October 1956, Israeli forces invaded Egypt's Sinai peninsula. Britain and France also responded to Egyptian nationalization of the Suez Canal by attacking Egypt. The UN stepped in, ending the fighting, arranging for foreign troops to leave Egyptian territory and setting up a peacekeeping force.

Egyptian president Gamal Abdel Nasser (1918–70) became leader of the Arab world after taking full control of the Suez Canal.

The Six-Day War

In 1967 Egypt again blocked Israeli shipping. Israel launched a surprise air attack on Egypt. Syria, Jordan and Iraq joined in on behalf of the Egyptians. Israel won the war in the air and on the ground, and six days later the UN arranged a ceasefire. Israel had again shown its military power and gained control of Sinai and the West Bank of the River Jordan.

In 1967 Israel took control of East Jerusalem. Israeli troops were able to parade in front of the Tower of David citadel.

THE FOUNDATION OF ISRAEL

1947
The UN agrees to divide Palestine into Arab and Jewish states and to place Jerusalem under international control.

1948
Foundation of the state of Israel; David Ben-Gurion becomes the nation's first prime minister.

1953–55
Moshe Sharett is Israeli prime minister, until Ben-Gurion takes over again.

1956
Egypt nationalizes the Suez Canal, leading to the Suez War, in which Britain and France help Israel.

1959
Israel starts a National Water Carrier Project to divert the River Jordan from the Sea of Galilee to the Negev region.

1967
The Six-Day War (June 5–10) between Israel and the Arab forces of Egypt, Iraq, Jordan and Syria; a UN resolution calls for the return of territory seized by Israel, recognition of Israel by the Arab states, free navigation, and future peace and stability.

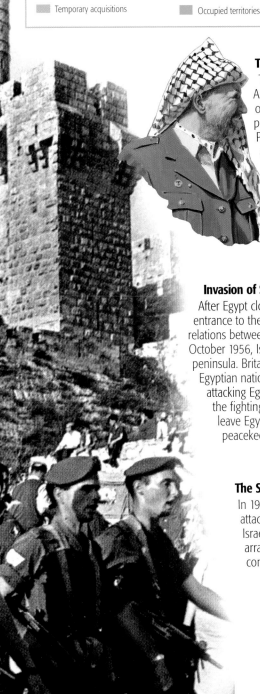

Europe Rises from the Ashes

Europe was at the center of the power struggle between the United States and the Soviet Union. The Cold War (see pages 10–11) resulted in the continent being strictly divided into West and East, and differences grew stronger throughout the 1950s. The new West Germany developed a strong economy under calm leadership. East Germany and the other Soviet satellite states did less well and were treated harshly whenever they rose up against their rulers.

A New Beginning

For Germany, the end of the war was a "zero hour"—time for a new beginning. By 1955, just six years after it was officially formed, the new West German republic had made remarkable progress. Chancellor Konrad Adenauer helped create an "economic miracle," which allowed ordinary Germans to improve their standard of living. Ruins had been cleared away and all the major cities were rebuilt, including Berlin. West Germany quickly became a successful consumer society, respected and integrated in post-war Western Europe.

Farming methods and foods such as milk products (right) were affected by the new policies.

Decolonization

Britain, France, the Netherlands and Portugal all had to come to terms with losing their overseas colonies. Between 1954 and 1962, there were bloody battles in Algeria, which fought for independence from France. In 1958 the former leader of the Free French, Charles de Gaulle, became president of France when there was almost civil war in his country over Algeria. He negotiated with nationalist leaders and ended French rule in Algeria four years later.

Creating a Common Market

In 1951, West Germany and five other nations (see Timeline, left) created a common market for coal, iron and steel. Seven years later this developed into the European Economic Community (EEC), which promoted economic cooperation among the six member countries. This included the free movement of workers between these countries, as well as joint policies on social welfare and foreign trade. In 1962 the EEC introduced a Common Agricultural Policy, which affected farming practice throughout Europe.

General Charles de Gaulle (1890–1970) became a symbol of France during his presidency (1958–69).

By the mid-1950s, Berlin was a bustling city again. The German motor industry was successful, and many people could afford their own family car.

NATO AND THE WARSAW PACT

West versus East

The North Atlantic Treaty Organization was formed in 1949 to resist any aggression by the Soviet Union. West Germany joined NATO in 1955. In response, in 1955 the Soviet Union set up a military alliance, the Warsaw Pact, with Albania, Bulgaria, Czechoslovakia, East Germany, Hungary, Poland, and Romania. It gave the Soviet Union even tighter control over its allies.

■ NATO nations ■ Warsaw Pact nations

■ Other US allies ■ Other USSR allies

The Soviets sent in tanks to put down the attempted revolution in Hungary.

Divided Continent

During the 1950s, Europe was divided into the capitalist West (including the Federal Republic of Germany) and the Communist East (including the German Democratic Republic). Western Europe was becoming more prosperous, but there were tensions in the Eastern bloc, where there were uprisings against strict Soviet rule. In Hungary, there was an attempted revolution by the people in 1956. When this was unsuccessful, the Hungarian prime minister and others were convicted of treason by the Soviets and executed.

Festival poster.

Post-War Britain

In the years immediately after the war, the Labor government turned Britain into a welfare state. The social security system helped working people, and many important industries were nationalized. During the 1950s, the Conservative government expanded the British economy and people had more money to spend. They enjoyed great national events, such as the Festival of Britain and the coronation of Elizabeth II. A sense of optimism and pride returned to British cultural life.

This toothpaste advertisement appeared in the Festival catalogue.

Festival of Britain

The Festival opened in May 1951 to demonstrate Britain's post-war development. The main exhibition was on the south bank of the Thames near Waterloo. It attracted more than 8 million visitors in less than 5 months. There were other sites in London, an exhibition of industrial power in Glasgow, as well as traveling exhibitions.

Queen Elizabeth's coronation was celebrated with street parties all over the country.

Crowds at the South Bank site in 1951. The Royal Festival Hall was built for the occasion.

Queen Elizabeth II enthroned, wearing the Diamond Diadem of 1820.

Queen's Coronation

Elizabeth II was crowned queen on 2 June, 1953. She drove with her husband, the Duke of Edinburgh, in a gold state coach from Buckingham Palace to Westminster Abbey, where the coronation service took place. Around 3 million people lined the streets of London to catch a glimpse of the queen. A further 27 million followed events on television, and for many Britons this was the first time they watched TV. Another 11 million listened on radio.

Consumer Comforts

By the 1950s, many people could afford more consumer goods. These included modern home conveniences, such as refrigerators, washing machines, and vacuum cleaners. They were followed in many homes by electrical entertainment items, including TV sets, better-quality radios, and record players. The design of these goods, and of homes in general, became more important in the 1960s.

New consumer goods were advertized as both useful and fun.

Immigrants in London in 1962, when a tough Commonwealth Immigrants Act made life more difficult for them.

POST-WAR BRITAIN

1945
The Labour Party wins the general election.

1948
The Empire Windrush docks in London, bringing hundreds of immigrants from the West Indies.

1949
Declaration of the independent Republic of Ireland; Northern Ireland remains part of the UK.

1951
The Conservatives return to power.

1952
King George VI dies; Elizabeth succeeds him.

1958
First CND march to the Atomic Weapons Research Establishment at Aldermaston.

1971
Decimal currency is introduced.

1972
The British government imposes direct rule of Northern Ireland from London.

Immigration

Post-war labor shortages in Britain led to immigrants being welcomed. Poles and Italians settled in the UK, followed by Commonwealth citizens from the West Indies. As immigration increased in the 1950s, there was racial tension and some violence. Race Relations Acts were passed in 1965 and 1968 to prevent discrimination. By 1971, however, the immigration laws had been tightened.

This CND marcher made his point with a stark question: "Which is to be banned? The bomb or the human."

Campaign for Nuclear Disarmament

The Campaign for Nuclear Disarmament (CND) was established in 1958, six years after Britain's first independent nuclear weapon test. The influential philosopher and social commentator Bertrand Russell was CND's president. The Campaign organized marches and demonstrations for the abandonment of nuclear weapons. It gained many supporters, as fears of a nuclear "World War III" grew more intense. There was also widespread concern at the environmental damage caused by atmospheric tests.

Northern Ireland

During the 1960s tension mounted in Northern Ireland, where working-class Catholics felt discriminated against, especially in jobs and housing. Civil rights demonstrations were followed by riots and violent clashes in Belfast and Londonderry. In 1969, extra British troops were sent to the province, where the pro-Catholic Irish Republican Army (IRA) and other militant organizations carried out bombings.

Burned-out vehicles were a common sight in Belfast during the height of the troubles.

中国
东方红

In 1956 the government simplified the characters of the Chinese written language.

Communist China

The Communists formed the People's Republic of China, uniting the country under a powerful central government. The defeated Nationalists were forced to form their own republic on the island of Taiwan. Mao Zedong introduced massive economic projects, some of which proved disastrous. Nevertheless, he was a strong leader with a cult following. After his death, economic conditions improved as China modernized and became more open to the world.

Students reading Mao's "Little Red Book." They and young Red Guards were encouraged always to carry a copy with them.

Mao Zedong (1893–1976) announced the birth of the People's Republic of China on 1 October 1949, in Beijing.

Chairman Mao

Mao Zedong, Chairman of the Communist Party, established the People's Republic of China in 1949. The new republic was run on similar political and social lines to the Soviet Union, with Mao and his party keeping a tight grip on people's lives. However, economic policies were not successful, and the collectivization of farming led to terrible famines in the late 1950s, in which millions starved.

Cultural Revolution

In 1966 Mao launched the Great Proletarian Cultural Revolution. Its stated aims were to get rid of bureaucracy and revive revolutionary attitudes. Leading officials were dismissed, universities were closed, and many intellectuals were sent to labor camps to be "re-educated." Many young people joined the Red Guards and attacked party officials who disagreed with Mao. The result was massive civil unrest, as the revolution turned into a reign of terror.

SPREAD OF COMMUNISM

AREAS CONTROLLED BY CHINESE COMMUNISTS:

- 1934
- 1936-1949
- By April 1947
- By July 1948
- By December 1949
- By 1950
- North Korea, occupied by Russia, 1945–48
- South Korea, occupied by US and UN, 1945–49
- Area controlled by Russia, 1945–48

SOVIET UNION
MONGOLIA
MANCHURIA
BEIJING
SHAANXI
CHINA
JIANGXI
TAIWAN

Nationalist Defeat

The map shows the steady growth of Communist control. Mao gained the support of vast numbers of peasants, as his army pushed the opposing Nationalists further south. At the end of 1949, Chiang Kai-shek and his Nationalist followers fled to Taiwan (previously called Formosa). There they set up a rival government for their own Republic of China.

Occupation of Tibet

Chinese forces moved in and occupied Tibet in 1950. The Tibetans surrendered their sovereignty to the Chinese government but kept their right to self-government and became an autonomous region of the People's Republic, called Xizang. An uprising in 1959 was suppressed, and Tibet's Buddhist spiritual and political leader, the Dalai Lama, fled to India. The Communists then repressed Tibetan culture.

New Beginning

In the early 1970s Mao's health failed, and he died in 1976. His widow Jiang Qing joined others in a so-called Gang of Four, but they failed to seize power. In 1977 the more moderate Deng Xiaoping became vice-chairman of the Communist Party and effectively leader of the republic. Deng was more liberal in running the economy and gave farming land back to the peasants. He also increased trade and contact with other countries.

The Dalai Lama has continued to oppose Chinese oppression. In 1989 he was awarded the Nobel Peace Prize.

不坚持社会开放，不发展经济，民生活，只能是死路

Deng Xiaoping (1904–97) is shown on this poster as a leader of economic reforms.

A brave protester tries to stop the tanks rolling into Tiananmen Square on 4 June 1989.

Planned Birth Policy

The government controlled all aspects of society. In 1979, it introduced a policy of limiting population growth. Couples were encouraged to have only one child; in some towns and cities this was a strict requirement. Later, rules were changed, so that families could have a second child if the first was a girl at least 3 years old. Offenders faced penalties, and many people considered this a violation of human rights.

Tiananmen Square

During the 1980s there were calls for a more democratic form of government, but attempts at political reform failed. In 1989 university students led crowds in large demonstrations in several Chinese cities. The biggest was in Tiananmen Square, in the capital, Beijing. Protesters called for more democracy and less corruption in government. Army tanks were sent in, and the peaceful protest was brutally put down. Hundreds of demonstrators were killed, and many more were arrested.

Posters promoted the two-parent, one-child family as ideal. Chinese authorities say the policy reduced the possible population by 300 million.

COMMUNIST CHINA

1946–49
Civil war between the Nationalists and Communists.

1958
The Great Leap Forward is introduced to increase industrial output, but fails.

1966–67
About 350 million copies of Quotations from Chairman Mao (the "Little Red Book") are published.

1971
The UN expels the Nationalists and admits the People's Republic as China's representative.

1972
US President Richard Nixon visits China and meets Mao and premier Zhou Enlai (1898–1976).

1979
China and the US establish normal diplomatic relations. Chinese border war with Vietnam.

1984
China reaches agreement with the UK for the return of Hong Kong in 1997.

1989
Tiananmen Square protest and massacre.

1991
China's first McDonald's burger restaurant opens in Beijing.

The Developing World

D uring the Cold War period, commentators often referred to the United States and other Western industrialized democracies as representing the First World. The Soviet Union and its satellites made up the Second World. The Third World referred to developing nations, most of which were former colonies of European nations. These poorer countries contained about three-quarters of the world's population.

Famine regularly struck millions of African children.

Poverty

There was an enormous divide between the "haves" of rich nations and the "have-nots" of the developing world. In the poorest countries, there was widespread hunger and disease, with a shortage of clean water and adequate shelter. There were few sources of energy, and illiteracy and poor equipment kept production down in agriculture and industry. Many people depended on a single crop, and if this failed, there was famine.

Revolutionary Shock Waves

Revolutions shook the world. A military coup in Egypt in 1952 led to the nationalization of the Suez Canal and an invasion by Israeli and Anglo-French forces. The UN settled the issue in Egypt's favor. Seven years later, Fidel Castro gained power in Cuba. Relations with the US quickly deteriorated, and the following year Cuba signed an economic pact with the Soviet Union.

The Suez Canal was extremely important to developed trading countries. The Egyptians decided to use the money it raised from the canal for an enormous hydroelectric dam.

Prime Minister Nasser of Egypt arrives at Bandung for the 1955 conference.

Bandung Conference

In 1955, India and four other nations organized a conference in Bandung, Indonesia. It was attended by 29 Asian and African countries, representing more than half the world's population. The developing countries expressed concern over tensions between the US and China, and dislike of colonialism. Over the next ten years, rich countries did give up some of their colonies, but the solidarity shown at Bandung gradually disappeared.

Nigerian troops on their way to fight supporters of an independent Biafra, in 1967. Three years later, Biafran resistance ended.

World Politics

The United States and the Soviet Union competed for influence in the developing world. Both superpowers wanted their political system to be the model for development in African countries. In 1972, for example, army leaders set up a Marxist-Leninist republic in Benin (then called Dahomey). In 1967, when Biafra tried to break away from Nigeria, the federal government was supported by the Soviet Union and Britain, while France helped the Biafran region.

THE DEVELOPING WORLD

1948
Mother Teresa starts her work for the poor of Calcutta.

1950
The Office of the United Nations High Commissioner for Refugees is established to resolve refugee problems worldwide.

1956
The US and UK withdraw financial support for the Aswan High Dam in Egypt, leading to the Suez Crisis; the Soviet Union later provides finance.

1956–75
Civil war rages in Angola, until final independence from Portugal.

1962
The UN World Food Program is established to provide food aid to people in need.

1968
Drought in the Sahel (Africa); 250,000 die.

1980
The World Health Organization announces the eradication of smallpox after mass vaccinations.

1991
Aung San Suu Kyi wins the Nobel Peace Prize for her efforts to restore democracy to Myanmar (Burma).

International Assistance

Charitable agencies were formed to provide relief and development aid for disaster-stricken communities. OXFAM (founded in 1942) worked on improving farming and food production in famine-stricken regions. Médecins Sans Frontières ("Doctors without borders") was set up in 1971 to provide emergency medical assistance. Unfortunately, the work of these and other agencies was often hampered by the governments of the countries in need.

Above: Mother Teresa (1910–97) founded a charity dedicated to helping the poor of Calcutta and other Indian cities.

Live Aid

Drought caused terrible famines in Ethiopia in 1984–85, killing about 1 million people. To raise money for the starving people of the region, rock singers and songwriters Bob Geldof and Midge Ure organized an all-day concert held at the same time in Philadelphia and London. The Live Aid concert was seen by an estimated 1.5 billion television viewers in 100 countries. It raised awareness of problems in the developing world, especially those caused by natural disasters.

Bob Geldof, lead singer of the Boomtown Rats, visited this Ethiopian famine-relief camp in January 1985.

AIDS Epidemic

The fatal disease AIDS (Acquired Immune Deficiency Syndrome) was first identified in 1981. It soon became epidemic throughout many developing regions, especially in Africa. According to the World Health Organization, by 1991 ten million people had AIDS, and a large proportion were in developing countries. Many were young adults, causing an overall decrease in life expectancy across Africa. By then the disease was being taken much more seriously in the US and other parts of the developed world.

In 1987, President Reagan described AIDS as "public enemy number one." The red ribbon was introduced in 1991 as a symbol of the fight against AIDS.

The Struggle for East and Southeast Asia

Communism and nationalism fuelled independence movements in the region. The tense Cold War atmosphere led to Soviet and China-backed regimes fighting those supported by the US and its allies. By the 1950s, France had lost control of Indo-China, and Vietnam became another battleground. The Vietnam War eventually led to massive anti-war demonstrations in the US and Europe, and the Americans were forced to withdraw.

Children throughout the region were forced to flee war.

Flashpoint Korea

After World War II, the Allies divided Korea. In 1950 North Korea, backed by China, invaded South Korea. The USA and UN countries came to the defence of the South. The Korean War lasted until 1953 without victory to either side and with more than 3 million people dead. The war also left the two countries separated by the world's most heavily fortified frontier.

American general Douglas MacArthur led South Korean, American, and United Nations troops in Korea.

WARTORN ASIA

1948
Foundation of North and South Korea.

1953
Cambodia and Laos gain independence from France.

1954
The Viet Minh take Dien Bien Phu from the French.

1963
Sabah, Sarawak and Singapore join Malaya to form the Federation of Malaysia.

1966
In Indonesia, Raden Suharto outlaws the Communist Party.

1967
The Association of Southeast Asian Nations (ASEAN) is founded to promote economic, cultural, and social cooperation.

1975
The Vietnam War ends.

1990
In Burma (Myanmar), the State Law and Order Restoration Council arrest Aung San Suu Kyi, leader of the National League for Democracy.

French Indo-China

France regained control of Indo-China—the region covering Cambodia, Laos and Vietnam—after World War II. But in 1946 war broke out between the French and revolutionary Vietnamese nationalists called the Viet Minh. By the time it ended, in 1954, Cambodia and Laos were already independent. According to the Geneva Agreements, Vietnam was temporarily divided at the 17th parallel, until national elections were held.

Monument to the Vietnamese Communist leader Ho Chi Minh (1890–1969), who became president of North Vietnam.

Vietnam War

The elections planned for Vietnam in 1954 never took place, and civil war broke out in South Vietnam. The United States sent military aid to the South Vietnamese government, while North Vietnam intervened on the side of the insurgents. US ground troops arrived in 1965, and the Soviet Union provided war materials for the North. Amidst growing opposition at home, the US withdrew its troops and North Vietnam eventually unified the country.

Cambodia

In 1975, Communists of the Khmer Rouge organization, led by Pol Pot, took control of Cambodia. Their ruthless policies were aimed at depriving people of their property and eliminating all opposition. Around 2 million Cambodians were executed or starved to death. An invading Vietnamese force overthrew Pol Pot in 1978, but the Khmer Rouge continued its guerrilla tactics. The Vietnamese left in 1989, but internal disagreements continued until 1991, when UN-led peace talks created a new coalition government.

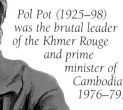

Pol Pot (1925–98) was the brutal leader of the Khmer Rouge and prime minister of Cambodia 1976–79.

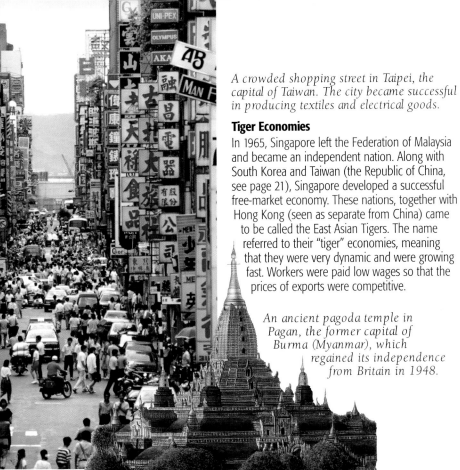

A crowded shopping street in Taipei, the capital of Taiwan. The city became successful in producing textiles and electrical goods.

Tiger Economies

In 1965, Singapore left the Federation of Malaysia and became an independent nation. Along with South Korea and Taiwan (the Republic of China, see page 21), Singapore developed a successful free-market economy. These nations, together with Hong Kong (seen as separate from China) came to be called the East Asian Tigers. The name referred to their "tiger" economies, meaning that they were very dynamic and were growing fast. Workers were paid low wages so that the prices of exports were competitive.

An ancient pagoda temple in Pagan, the former capital of Burma (Myanmar), which regained its independence from Britain in 1948.

SOUTHEAST ASIA, 1946–75

INDIA 1947
BHUTAN
PEOPLE'S REPUBLIC OF CHINA
MYANMAR (BURMA) 1948
BANGLADESH (EAST PAKISTAN) 1947
NORTH VIETNAM, 1954
SOUTH VIETNAM 1954
PHILIPPINES 1946
LAOS 1954
SRI LANKA (CEYLON), 1947
CAMBODIA 1954
MALAYA, 1957
SINGAPORE, 1965
INDONESIA, 1949

Divided Nations

The map shows Southeast Asian dates of independence. In Burma, civil war ended when a bloodless coup set up a ruling revolutionary council of military leaders in 1962. In 1976, North and South Vietnam unified into a single nation, the Socialist Republic of Vietnam, with its capital at Hanoi.

US marines on a "search and destroy" ground mission near the village of Tam Ky in South Vietnam in 1968.

Winds of Change in Africa

Algerian Conflict

France had governed much of Algeria since 1830. Many French and other European citizens had settled there, and Algerians were subjects of France. It was a most important colony, four times the size of the mother country. Independence was gained only after an 8-year long conflict between Algerian nationalists and France (see page 17), where there were many differing attitudes towards colonialism.

Women were recruited to fight for Algerian independence by the National Liberation Front (FLN).

During the early 1950s, African political parties increased their demands for freedom for their nations. Rapidly growing nationalism took the colonizing countries by surprise. In 1960 alone, 17 new independent countries came into being. By the 1970s there were few colonies left, mostly in the southern region. There, white colonial governments found it increasingly difficult to resist the black African majority.

Kenya and the Mau Mau

Kenya had been a British colony since 1920. In the 1950s a secret independence movement of the Kenyan Kikuyu people led a revolt against the colonial government. Members of this nationalist movement, called the Mau Mau by Europeans, were considered terrorists by the British. Thousands of nationalists were put in detention camps, and more than 13,000 Africans were killed during the conflict.

Jomo Kenyatta (1891–1978), leader of the Kenya African Union, is led to trial in 1952. He was jailed for 7 years for his part in the Mau Mau rebellion.

Apartheid in South Africa

Apartheid (Afrikaans for "separateness") was a system of racial segregation introduced by the ruling National Party in 1948. The system classified South Africans in four groups—white, black, colored, (mixed race) and Asian. The groups were segregated in education, housing and transport. The African National Congress (ANC) fought for equal rights for blacks, but was declared illegal, and some leaders, including Nelson Mandela, were jailed. Apartheid finally ended in 1991.

ANC members demonstrated against apartheid and demanded the release of Nelson Mandela, who spent 27 years in jail.

This poster captured African feelings of the 1950s.

South of the Sahara

In 1957, the Gold Coast was the first black African colony to become independent, leaving the British Commonwealth and taking the name Ghana. Three years later, all its immediate neighbors gained independence from France—Burkina Faso (formerly French West Africa), Côte d'Ivoire and Togo (French Togoland). By the mid-1960s, many sub-Saharan nations had gained their independence without conflict, and Belgium, Britain, and France had given up most of their African colonies.

A military band in Gabon (formerly French Equatorial Africa) celebrates independence in 1960.

The Belgian Congo became independent Congo in 1960 (renamed Zaïre in 1971).

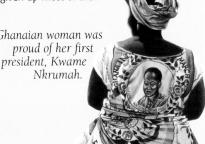

This Ghanaian woman was proud of her first president, Kwame Nkrumah.

Coups and Civil War

A number of newly independent countries soon faced internal conflicts. Five years after independence, a military coup overthrew the government of the Central African Republic. In Nigeria, the region of Biafra attempted to break away in 1967. In Uganda, a military coup brought Idi Amin to power in 1971. His brutal regime lasted for 8 years, until he was overthrown by Ugandan exiles and Tanzanian troops.

After his coup, Idi Amin (1925–2003) had himself sworn in as president of Uganda.

ALL MEN ARE BORN EQUAL

AFRICAN INDEPENDENCE, 1974–90

1. Guinea-Bissau (1974)
2. Angola (1975)
3. Mozambique (1975)
4. Cape Verde (1975)
5. Comoros (1975)
6. Sao Tome & Principe (1975)
7. Djibouti (1977)
8. Zimbabwe (1980)
9. Namibia (1990)

START OF INDEPENDENCE

1951 *Libya (from Italy).*

1956 *Morocco (France), Sudan (UK), Tunisia (France).*

1957 *Ghana (UK).*

1958 *Guinea (France).*

1960 *Benin (France), Burkina Faso (France), Cameroon (France, UK), Central African Republic (France), Chad (France), Congo (France), Côte d'Ivoire (France), DR Congo (Belgium), Gabon (France), Madagascar (France), Mali (France), Mauritania (France), Niger (France), Nigeria (UK), Senegal (France), Somalia (Italy, UK), Togo (France).*

1961 *Sierra Leone (UK), Tanzania (UK).*

1962 *Algeria (France), Burundi (Belgium), Rwanda (Belgium), Uganda (UK).*

1963 *Kenya (UK).*

1964 *Malawi (UK), Zambia (UK).*

1965 *Botswana (UK), Gambia (UK).*

1966 *Lesotho (UK).*

1968 *Equatorial Guinea (Spain), Mauritius (UK), Swaziland (UK).*

Liberation Movements
Determined liberation movements at last achieved independence for large parts of southern Africa during the 1970s. There was civil war in Angola and a long period of guerrilla warfare in Mozambique before freedom was gained. South Africa's control over Namibia was finally ended, just 4 years before the South Africans themselves enjoyed majority rule.

The USA: Confrontation and Civil Rights

In the 1950s, southern states still practised racial segregation.

While the Cold War continued, racial discrimination became a controversial issue in the United States. The civil rights movement grew dramatically throughout the 1950s, as leading African Americans became more influential. There were riots and shootings, but new laws in the 1960s led to greater integration. By then the Vietnam War had become another major issue for students and other protesters, who wanted an end to violence and warfare.

John F. Kennedy (1917–63) (below), with his wife Jacqueline. Front-page report (right) of the assassination.

JFK Assassinated

President John F. Kennedy was killed by an assassin's bullet on 22 November 1963, at a very tense period of the Cold War. At the time some people suspected that the Cubans or Russians must have been involved in the murder plot. If that had been the case, the next president, Lyndon B. Johnson, might well have come to the conclusion that a nuclear war was inevitable.

Martin Luther King (1929–68) in Washington in 1963, when more than 200,000 people staged a freedom march.

Struggle for Civil Rights

Baptist minister Martin Luther King was an activist in the US South who became a national leader of the civil rights movement. In 1963 he made a famous speech, in which he said he had a dream that his children "will one day live in a nation where they will not be judged by the color of their skin but by the content of their character."

Protests and Demonstrations

In the 1960s, students and others staged bigger and better organized boycotts, demonstrations, marches and sit-ins for civil rights and against war. Folk singers wrote protest songs, and the youth movement included hippies, who believed in "flower power" and a world based on love and peace. Different groups were brought together by their opposition to the Vietnam War (see page 24), which they felt showed the United States in its worst light.

Journalists at the Washington Post (above) exposed the Watergate scandal. President Richard Nixon (1913–94) (right) at first denied any involvement.

Watergate

In 1972, Republican Party employees were found to have broken into Democratic Party headquarters at the Watergate building in Washington DC. This was part of a secret and illegal campaign to help Richard Nixon win the 1972 presidential election. The break-in was covered up, as the White House denied all knowledge of the affair. It eventually became clear that Nixon had been involved, and the president resigned in August 1974. He was pardoned by the next president, Gerald Ford.

Malcolm X (1925–65), born Malcolm Little in Nebraska, was assassinated while addressing a rally in New York.

Malcolm X

The civil rights leader Malcolm X was originally an influential member of the militant Black Muslims, or Nation of Islam movement, which believed in black power and aimed to establish an Islamic state. In 1964 Malcolm X (whose initial stood for the unknown name of his African ancestors) visited Mecca and then founded his own Organization of Afro-American Unity. He was condemned as a hypocrite and shot by Black Muslim militants.

MAI 68

DÉBUT D'UNE
LUTTE
PROLONGÉE

So-called "flower children" preached gentleness and love, but they were also prepared to speak out against war and racial discrimination.

International Superstars

The biggest star of the new rock 'n' roll music that appeared in the 1950s was Elvis Presley, who had a string of chart-topping hits on both sides of the Atlantic. He was followed by a number of American and, in the 1960s, British singers and groups. The new superstars also made films, just as some film stars made records.

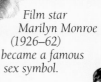

Elvis Presley (1935–77) had his first big hit in 1956 with "Heartbreak Hotel."

Jimi Hendrix (1942–70), the great American rock-music guitarist.

Film star Marilyn Monroe (1926–62) became a famous sex symbol.

The Beatles, from Liverpool, shot to fame in 1962 with "Love Me Do."

New Look

French fashion designer Christian Dior (1905–57) introduced his first collection in 1947. Called the New Look, it included narrow waists and extravagantly full, long skirts, with elegant accessories. As with other designers, Dior's business expanded into jewelry and perfumes, to complete the "look," which was taken up by American film stars. The short miniskirt came as a complete contrast in the 1960s.

An elegant New Look ball gown of 1949.

Pop Art

The movement known as pop art originated in the 1950s in Britain, and then developed in the United States. Artists such as Andy Warhol and Roy Lichtenstein were inspired by mass media images of television, comics, and advertising to break down the barriers between high art and popular culture. The movement was also a reaction to the earlier abstract expressionism of artists such as Jackson Pollock.

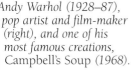

Andy Warhol (1928–87), pop artist and film-maker (right), and one of his most famous creations, Campbell's Soup (1968).

Spy Thrillers

The realities of World War II and the Cold War led to an interest in fiction set in the world of espionage, intelligence agencies and secret services. The dangerous, violent aspects of spying were mixed with a fascination for secret codes and false identities. The fictional character of James Bond, created by writer Ian Fleming (1908–64), became an international icon through a series of books and films.

James Bond appeared first in the book Casino Royale (1953) and on screen in the film Dr No (1962).

Icons, Idols, and Trends

The post-war consumer boom brought massive changes in popular culture. Rock 'n' roll and other forms of modern music spread from the United States. Successful pop and film stars became global idols, influencing the way young people dressed and behaved. Pop artists also reacted against the past, as the rich countries of the world entered the "swinging sixties." At the same time, feminists rebelled against women's traditional, conventional roles. Pop culture became a search for freedom.

Hippie Culture

The hippie movement of 1960s America, which included non-violent protest against war and nuclear arms (see pages 28–29), spread to Europe and elsewhere. Hippie culture, associated with drugs such as marijuana and LSD, influenced pop music and street fashion and promoted a liberal attitude towards "free love." It coincided with the rise of the "women's lib" movement, which sought equal opportunities for women, free contraception, and abortion on demand.

Carnaby Street, London West End.

Religious Cults

Several new religious groups gained popularity during the 1960s. The International Society for Krishna Consciousness, popularly known as the Hare Krishna movement, spread from India. Members wearing orange robes were often seen chanting in the streets. Transcendental Meditation also came from India, and gained in popularity after the Beatles met its guru, Maharishi Mahesh Yogi, in 1967. In the 1970s, members of the Unification Church, called Moonies after their founder Sun Myung Moon, tried to spread belief in a global struggle between good and evil.

A Hare Krishna member with the group's 16-word mantra, which is supposed to bring about a higher state of spiritual awareness.

Carnaby Street, in London's West End, became famous for its fashionable shops and represented trendy life in the "swinging sixties."

The Space Race

The United States and the Soviet Union both used their developments and successes in space technology as Cold War propaganda tools. The wish to demonstrate superiority became more intense after the Soviet launch of the first satellite, causing a genuine "space race." After early Soviet successes, the US won the competition to land a man on the Moon, before putting its efforts into reusable shuttle technology.

G-2, the first Soviet intermediate range ballistic missile (IRBM), launched in 1949.

Guided Missiles

The superpowers raced to produce guided missiles for military purposes. In 1957, the Soviets tested their R-7, the first intercontinental ballistic missile (ICBM). Four months later, the US had a similar Atlas-A. ICBMs could send a nuclear warhead more than 15,000 km (9,300 mi). During the 1960s, as the number of attacking missiles increased, both superpowers developed anti-ballistic missile systems.

THE SPACE RACE

1958
The US launches its first satellites and establishes the National Aeronautics and Space Administration (NASA).

1961
A month after Yuri Gagarin's space flight, US astronaut Alan Shepard travels in space for 15 minutes in Mercury 3.

1962
John Glenn is the first US astronaut to orbit Earth.

1971
The first space station, Salyut 1, is launched by the Soviet Union.

1972
Apollo 17 is the last Apollo mission to the Moon.

1975
A US Apollo spacecraft docks with a Soviet Soyuz craft in space.

1983
A Pioneer 10 probe becomes the first manmade object to leave the solar system.

1986
Space shuttle Challenger explodes soon after launch, killing all 7 crew.

1987–88
Russian cosmonauts spend nearly a year in the Mir space station.

1989
Voyager 2 probe reaches Neptune after 12 years.

Into Orbit

In 1957, the Soviet R-7 rocket sent the first artificial satellite into space. *Sputnik 1* orbited the Earth for three months. While it was in space, the Soviets launched *Sputnik 2*, which carried a dog. The Soviet Vostok and US Mercury programs raced to get a human into space. On 12 April 1961, the Russian Yuri Gagarin made the first successful orbit in *Vostok 1.*

The first animal in space was Laika the dog. Sadly, she did not survive the flight.

A Mercury space capsule, which took the first American into space in 1961.

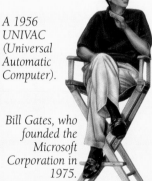

A 1956 UNIVAC (Universal Automatic Computer).

Bill Gates, who founded the Microsoft Corporation in 1975.

Computer Age

Developments in the field of computers helped space travel. Early machines filled whole rooms, but in 1959 IBM introduced its first transistorized computer. This led to the introduction of minicomputers. As computers got smaller, they also became more powerful, until the first personal computer (PC) was launched in 1975.

A 1980s virtual reality headset.

Shuttles

In 1981, NASA launched its first space shuttle, named *Columbia*. It was able to travel in space and land on Earth again many times. By 1991 there had been a further 43 flights by four different shuttles. They were used to deploy satellites, probes, the Hubble space telescope and the Spacelab station. In 1984, shuttle astronauts captured and repaired a satellite in space.

Space shuttle Atlantis is carried back to Kennedy Space Center after landing in California.

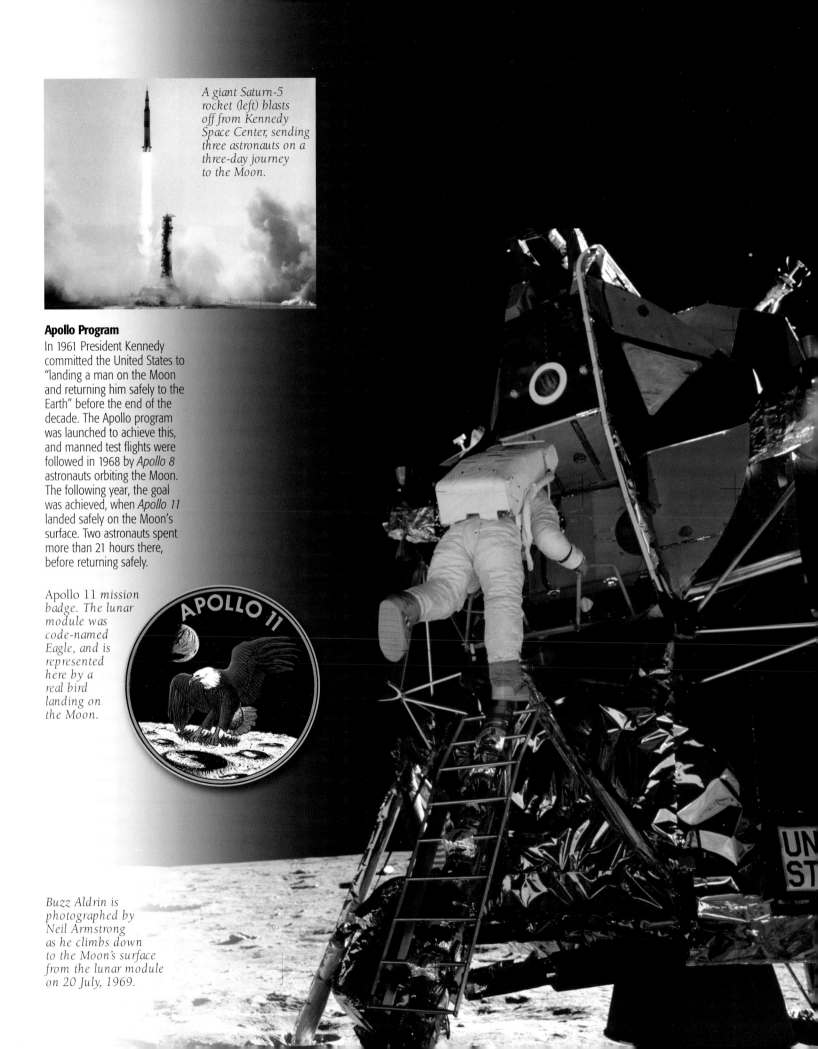

A giant Saturn-5 rocket (left) blasts off from Kennedy Space Center, sending three astronauts on a three-day journey to the Moon.

Apollo Program

In 1961 President Kennedy committed the United States to "landing a man on the Moon and returning him safely to the Earth" before the end of the decade. The Apollo program was launched to achieve this, and manned test flights were followed in 1968 by *Apollo 8* astronauts orbiting the Moon. The following year, the goal was achieved, when *Apollo 11* landed safely on the Moon's surface. Two astronauts spent more than 21 hours there, before returning safely.

Apollo 11 mission badge. The lunar module was code-named Eagle, and is represented here by a real bird landing on the Moon.

Buzz Aldrin is photographed by Neil Armstrong as he climbs down to the Moon's surface from the lunar module on 20 July, 1969.

Revolts in Central and South America

A South American guerrilla fighter (the Spanish word means "small war").

US capitalist interests and Communist ideology had a profound influence on many Latin American countries during the Cold War. Nationalism added tension to this dangerous mix, leading to army-backed dictatorships in the largest countries—Brazil and Argentina—as well as many others. Repression of any form of opposition led to enormous numbers being tortured and killed, or going missing. Democratically elected governments returned toward the end of the period.

Monument in Grenada to the successful US invasion of 1983.

Grenada
Former British colony Grenada, in the West Indies, was taken over by a rebel Marxist leader in 1979. Four years later there was another uprising by left-wing forces. The US, contending that the island was becoming a Communist outpost, invaded and installed a new government. Elections were held the following year.

A ship passes through the narrowest section of the Panama Canal.

Civil War in Nicaragua
For more than 40 years Nicaragua was dominated by the Somoza family. Opposition to this regime finally brought civil war in 1976–79, forcing the exile of President Somoza Debayle. The new government was headed by the Sandinista National Liberation Front. From 1981 to 1990 the US backed a coalition of anti-Sandinista forces, called the Contras, while the Soviet Union supported the government. The Sandinistas lost power in elections in 1990.

Panama Canal
In the 1970s, there was a movement in Panama to end US control of the Canal. In 1977 the two countries signed a treaty, agreeing a transfer of the Canal Zone in 1979 and full Panamanian control of the Canal itself 20 years later. The US was very concerned at the actions of General Noriega, head of the Panamanian forces. After Noriega forced his president from office and declared elections invalid, the Americans sent in a force to capture him. A convicted drug-trafficker, he was imprisoned.

A soldier in the Nicaraguan civil war. It has been estimated that 60,000 died in the struggle in the 1980s.

CENTRAL AND SOUTH AMERICA, 1982

MEXICO
HONDURAS CUBA HAITI
BELIZE DOMINICAN REPUBLIC
PORTO RICO
GUATEMALA JAMAICA
EL SALVADOR NICARAGUA GUYANA
COSTA RICA SURINAME
PANAMA FRENCH
COLOMBIA GUYANA
ECUADOR
BRAZIL
PERU
BOLIVIA
CHILE PARAGUAY
ARGENTINA URUGUAY

- ■ USA and allies
- ■ American military assistance
- ■ Soviet ally
- ■ Soviet military assistance
- ■ Other Western military assistance
- ■ French military presence

Cold War Struggles
The two superpowers struggled to gain the upper hand in this region. In the early 1960s, there was a series of crises surrounding Cuba, which took the US and the USSR to the brink of nuclear war. In the 1970s, US neighbor Mexico decided to improve relations with Cuba and Chile despite US opposition. The map shows the situation in 1982.

Argentinean Nationalism

After Juan Perón's second period as president of Argentina (1973–74), the economic situation got worse. Military juntas took over the running of the country from 1976 to 1983, a period of authoritarian rule and political terrorism. Around 20,000 Argentineans may have been killed in the so-called "dirty war." Having lost the Falklands War against the UK in 1982, Argentina democratically elected a new president the following year.

The cathedral in the modern city of Brasilia, which replaced Rio de Janeiro as Brazil's capital in 1960.

Eva (Evita) Perón (1919–52), second wife of the Argentinean president, introduced many reforms. She famously addressed the crowds from the balcony of the Casa Rosada (Pink House), the country's presidential palace.

Brazil's Military Rule

South America's largest republic came under military rule after a coup in 1964. Over the next 21 years, a series of authoritarian regimes failed to improve the economic situation, which included high inflation and labor unrest. Towards the end of the period, there were calls for political rights for ordinary people, and in 1985 a civilian president was elected.

Augusto Pinochet (1915–2006), right, on a visit to Santiago, Paraguay, in 1974 to visit another president and military dictator, Alfredo Stroessner (1912–2006), seated.

Changes in Chile

In 1970 Salvador Allende, a Marxist, was elected president of Chile and started a socialist program, including nationalization of the country's copper mines. He was overthrown by a military coup three years later, which led to violent struggles, causing thousands of deaths and the emigration of many. General Augusto Pinochet ruled over a repressive regime until 1990, when civilian, democratic government was at last restored.

US–Soviet Stand-Off

Relations between the two world superpowers changed throughout the Cold War. Tensions rose and fell after the death of Stalin, as one side responded to actions—or intended actions—by the other. The Cuban missile crisis of 1962 led the superpowers and the world to the brink of nuclear war. The policy of brinkmanship was an extremely dangerous one. Events in Hungary and Czechoslovakia also showed that the Soviets would not tolerate a weakening of the Communist system.

Nikita Khrushchev (1894–1971) denounced Stalin in 1956 for his "intolerance, brutality and abuse of power."

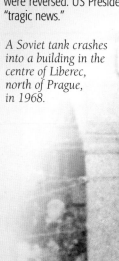

Post-Stalin Thaw

Soviet leader Khrushchev believed in the superiority of the Communist system and felt that it would overtake western capitalism in time. Nevertheless, he and President Eisenhower agreed at a meeting in Geneva in 1955 that a nuclear war would be disastrous for everyone. The following year, Khrushchev began a program of "destalinization," discrediting the former leader and calling for peaceful coexistence between East and West. Yet just six years later, there was a missile crisis (see page 37).

Soviet–China Split

Relations between the Soviet Union and China worsened in the late 1950s. The Chinese felt the Russians were becoming soft towards the West. The Soviets were alarmed by the failed campaign of China's "Great Leap Forward." In 1961, Chinese prime minister Zhou Enlai left the 22nd Communist Party Congress in Moscow abruptly. Eight years later, fighting broke out between the two countries over a border dispute.

A Soviet poster of 1950 shows Stalin greeting Mao Zedong. This apparent solidarity was a great worry to the United States.

ПУСТЬ ЖИВЕТ И КРЕПНЕТ НЕРУШИМАЯ ДРУЖБА И СОТРУДНИЧЕСТВО СОВЕТСКОГО И КИТАЙСКОГО НАРОДОВ!

Prague Spring

Alexander Dubcek became secretary of the Czechoslovak Communist Party in 1968. During a period known as the Prague Spring, he introduced liberal reforms. The Soviets were unhappy at this, fearing that it weakened their control in Czechoslovakia and their position in the Cold War world. Soviet and other Warsaw Pact troops invaded Czechoslovakia and occupied Prague. Dubcek was ousted and his reforms were reversed. US President Johnson called the invasion "tragic news."

A Soviet tank crashes into a building in the centre of Liberec, north of Prague, in 1968.

A Cuban exile in the USA watches news of the developing missile crisis.

Signs of Détente

By the mid-1970s, after the first Strategic Arms Limitation Treaty, there was a slight relaxation in Cold War tensions. At a Conference on Security and Cooperation in Europe (CSCE), the two superpowers and 33 other nations agreed to recognize the European boundaries that had been set up after World War II. These included the Baltic states annexed by the Soviets. All parties also agreed to respect human rights and improve cultural and economic cooperation.

Soviet leader Leonid Brezhnev (1906–82) signs the CSCE Final Act in Helsinki, 1975.

Cuban Missile Crisis

In 1962, the US discovered that Soviet nuclear missiles were being installed in Cuba. President Kennedy demanded that Khrushchev remove the missiles and dismantle the bases, and the US blockaded Soviet shipments to Cuba. For six days the world was on the brink of a possible nuclear war, until the Soviet leader accepted Kennedy's demands in return for a US undertaking not to attack Cuba.

Signs such as this became increasingly common in the 1970s.

The Reagan–Thatcher Years

Margaret Thatcher was the longest serving British prime minister of the 20th century. During the 1980s, her period in office coincided with that of US President Ronald Reagan. The two leaders' shared economic beliefs meant that Reaganomics, as they became known, were not very different from Thatcherism. There were differences of approach and opinion—over the Falklands War and the US invasion of Grenada, for example—but the president and prime minister were seen by the world as allies and friends.

Ronald Reagan and Margaret Thatcher at Camp David, Maryland, in 1986.

Economic problems

Both the US and UK suffered economic difficulties throughout the 1970s. There were growing problems of inflation, strikes and fuel shortages. In 1973, the member states of the Organization of Petroleum Exporting Countries (including Iraq, Saudi Arabia, and Venezuela) disagreed with major oil companies. OPEC raised crude oil prices by up to 200 percent, causing a sharp rise in petrol and other prices in the USA and the UK, and triggering an economic recession.

The Prince and Princess of Wales rode in an open-topped state landau from the cathedral to Buckingham Palace.

The Royal Wedding

On 29 July 1981, hundreds of thousands of people lined the streets of London to see Prince Charles, heir to the British throne, and Lady Diana Spencer on their wedding day. The marriage took place at St. Paul's Cathedral, watched by a television audience of 750 million people around the world. The bride became the Princess of Wales.

Conservative Policies

Ronald Reagan's Republican administration and Margaret Thatcher's Conservative government had similar aims and policies. Reagan wanted to cut taxes, reduce welfare benefits and increase spending on defense. His economic program became known as Reaganomics. Both leaders believed in free enterprise and opposed the state regulation of business, but economic downturns in the late 1980s prevented them from carrying through all their policies. In foreign affairs, they both took a hard line on the Soviet Union.

Iraqi forces set fire to oil wells outside Kuwait City before withdrawing from the region. They also dumped oil into the Persian Gulf.

War in the Falklands

In April 1982, Argentinean troops invaded the Falkland Islands, a British overseas territory in the South Atlantic. Attempts by the United Nations and the US to find a peaceful solution to the differences failed, and Britain sent ships, planes and 6,000 troops to the islands. By June the UK had won the war, but more than 900 soldiers died in the conflict.

A British Royal Navy commando in the Falklands (left). The reputation of Margaret Thatcher (right) was boosted at home by patriotic sentiment and a sense of victory.

From Punks to Yuppies

Punk rock of the late 1970s was an aggressive, rebellious form of popular music that influenced youth culture and fashion. It encouraged extreme hair-dos and body piercing. In the 1980s, rap music became more popular. The consumer boom also produced so-called yuppies (young urban professionals)– who were earning a lot of money and enjoyed spending it.

In 1983, consumers queued to buy "adoptable" Cabbage Patch Kids dolls.

Yuppies had plenty of money to spend.

Piercings and wild hair-dos were part of punk style.

Mobile phones were an innovation.

The Gulf War

After Iraq–led by Saddam Hussein–invaded Kuwait in August 1990, a coalition force of the US and UN countries (including the UK) launched Operation Desert Storm in January 1991. This included massive air attacks from Saudi Arabia, followed by a ground offensive. The Iraqis left Kuwait at the end of February 1991 and were forced to agree to comply with UN resolutions. Nevertheless, tensions continued between Iraq and the US.

THE REAGAN-THATCHER YEARS

1973
UK joins the European Economic Community.

1976
A Soviet newspaper calls Margaret Thatcher the "Iron Lady."

1979–90
Margaret Thatcher is the first female Prime Minister of the United Kingdom.

1981–89
Ronald Reagan is 40th President of the USA.

1981
Race riots in Britain. Reagan is shot in a failed assassination attempt.

1983
Reagan announces the Strategic Defense Initiative (SDI or "Star Wars").

1984
Miners' strike in Britain, as coal mines are closed.

1987
On Black Monday (Oct 19), world stock market prices show the biggest single-day drop (23 per cent in US).

1990
Anti-poll tax riots in UK.

1991
Margaret Thatcher is awarded the US Presidential Medal of Freedom.

A Russian doll shows the figures of Lenin, Stalin, Brezhnev, Gorbachev, and Yeltsin.

Soviet Collapse

By the mid-1980s, the cost of maintaining a massive military machine was ruining the Soviet economy. Mikhail Gorbachev brought in reforms, but they were too few, too late. The Soviets were forced to allow non-Communist governments to come to power in their Eastern European satellites. Their own republics started declaring independence and, at the end of 1991, the Soviet Union ceased to exist.

Everyday goods were often in short supply in the Soviet Union in the 1980s. People had to queue outside shops.

War in Afghanistan

In December 1979, Soviet troops invaded Afghanistan, which bordered on its three southernmost republics. They did so in order to support the Marxist revolutionary council that had taken over against its many opponents. Opposition rebel guerrillas called mujahedin ("holy warriors") believed that the new government's policies went against the teachings of Islam. The Soviets fought for nine years, before withdrawing in 1988–89.

An Afghan rebel soldier. The mujahedin were supplied with US arms via Pakistan.

Economic Problems

The Soviet economy did not make any progress under Brezhnev in the late 1970s. The government invested huge sums in farming and agricultural equipment, but output went down. This meant the Soviets had to import large amounts of grain, which they could only afford because of an expansion in their oil and gas industries. The US protested against the invasion of Afghanistan by limiting supplies of its wheat to the Soviet Union, which made matters worse.

People of all ages helped knock down parts of the Berlin Wall in 1989. Some kept pieces as souvenirs.

Fall of the Berlin Wall

The Berlin Wall had stood since 1961 as a symbol of the political conflict between East and West. In 1989, Hungary opened its border with Austria, allowing thousands of East Germans to move through Austria to West Germany. Anti-government demonstrations broke out in East Germany, and it was finally announced that East Germans could travel freely. Thousands of people flooded the checkpoints and the Berlin Wall was opened.

Soviet Republics

The USSR was made up of 15 socialist republics, of which Russia was by far the biggest, followed by the Kazakh and Ukrainian republics. The three Baltic republics were annexed in 1940, when the Moldavian republic was also created. In 1990 Lithuania was the first republic to declare its independence.

Cotton is an important crop in the Central Asian republics.

An Uzbek man.

LITHUANIA is KUVEIT 1940 !

A Lithuanian protester.

A Kyrgyz man celebrates independence.

Soviet passports skewered on Lithuanian railings.

Street scene in a Moscow suburb during the 1980s. The new reforms did not have an immediate effect on most people's everyday lives.

Glasnost and Perestroika

When Gorbachev became head of the Soviet Communist Party in 1985, he set about trying to improve the economy through a policy of *perestroika* ("restructuring") aimed at increasing efficiency. Gorbachev's *glasnost* ("openness") policy tried to make Soviet society freer and more flexible. These initiatives were not popular with old-fashioned Communists. The reforms, though many failed, nevertheless encouraged freedom movements within many of the 15 republics that made up the Union.

INDEPENDENT STATES, 1991

1 Lithuania	3 Estonia	6 Moldova
2 Latvia	4 Belarus	7 Georgia
	5 Ukraine	8 Armenia

RUSSIAN FEDERATION

9 Azerbaijan	11 Uzbekistan	13 Kyrgyzstan
10 Turkmenistan	12 Tajikistan	14 Kazakhstan

End of the USSR

In December 1991, Russia, Belarus, and Ukraine announced that the Soviet Union was no more and formed a new Commonwealth of Independent States. Eight other newly independent states quickly joined this loose confederation, but the Baltic States (1, 2 and 3 on the map) did not. On 25 December, the Soviet flag was lowered in Moscow and the USSR ceased to exist.

Chernobyl

On 26 April 1986, a reactor failed in a run-down nuclear power station at Chernobyl in the Ukrainian republic. The reactor should have shut down automatically, but a safety device had been switched off. There was a massive explosion that blew the top off the reactor, causing the world's worst nuclear accident. Many thousands were killed or made seriously ill by the nuclear fallout in Ukraine, neighboring republics and much further afield.

The Chernobyl disaster convinced many people that nuclear power is dangerous.

SOVIET COLLAPSE

1982–84
Yuri Andropov (1914–84) is president.

1984–85
Konstantin Chernenko (1911–85) is president.

1985
Chernenko is succeeded by Mikhail Gorbachev.

1987
Boris Yeltsin (1931–2007) is dismissed as Moscow party chief for criticizing the slow pace of reforms.

1989
First openly contested elections are held for the newly created Congress of Peoples' Deputies.

1990
The Soviet government votes to permit non-Communist political parties.

1991
In July, Gorbachev and President Bush sign START (the Strategic Arms Reduction Treaty). In August, Boris Yeltsin opposes a conservative coup against Gorbachev. On 25 December, Gorbachev resigns as Soviet president. On 26 December, the Russian government takes over offices of the former USSR.

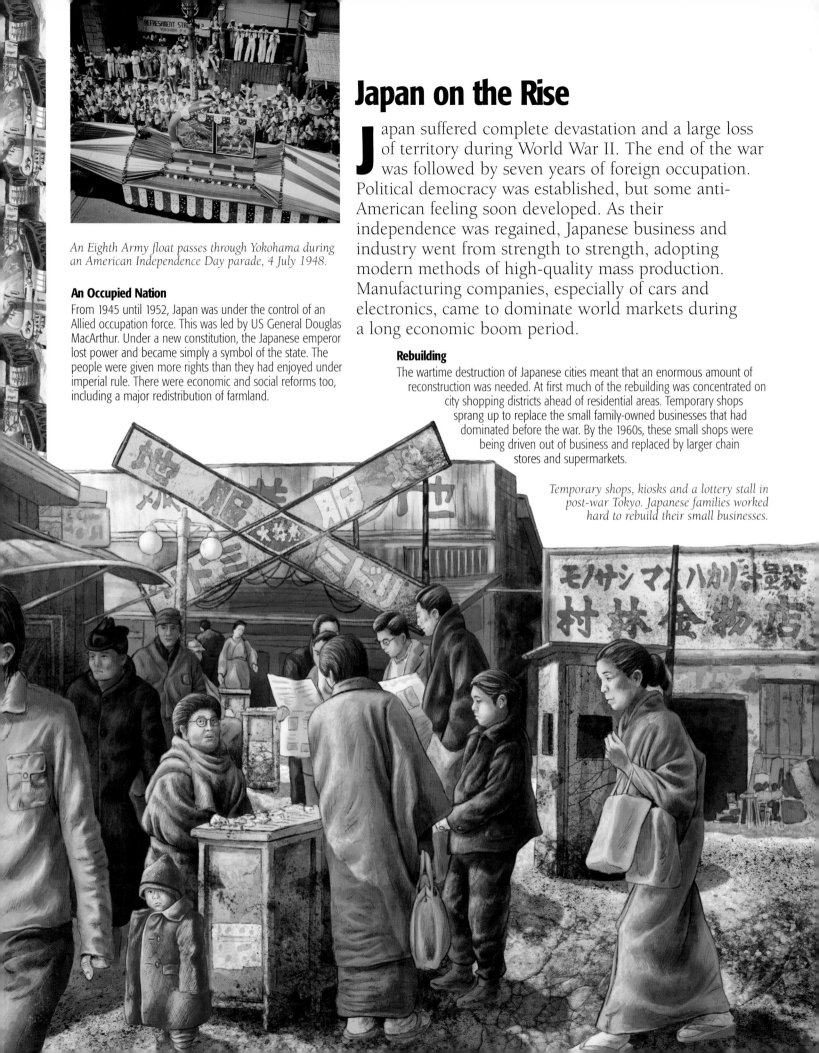

Japan on the Rise

Japan suffered complete devastation and a large loss of territory during World War II. The end of the war was followed by seven years of foreign occupation. Political democracy was established, but some anti-American feeling soon developed. As their independence was regained, Japanese business and industry went from strength to strength, adopting modern methods of high-quality mass production. Manufacturing companies, especially of cars and electronics, came to dominate world markets during a long economic boom period.

An Eighth Army float passes through Yokohama during an American Independence Day parade, 4 July 1948.

An Occupied Nation

From 1945 until 1952, Japan was under the control of an Allied occupation force. This was led by US General Douglas MacArthur. Under a new constitution, the Japanese emperor lost power and became simply a symbol of the state. The people were given more rights than they had enjoyed under imperial rule. There were economic and social reforms too, including a major redistribution of farmland.

Rebuilding

The wartime destruction of Japanese cities meant that an enormous amount of reconstruction was needed. At first much of the rebuilding was concentrated on city shopping districts ahead of residential areas. Temporary shops sprang up to replace the small family-owned businesses that had dominated before the war. By the 1960s, these small shops were being driven out of business and replaced by larger chain stores and supermarkets.

Temporary shops, kiosks and a lottery stall in post-war Tokyo. Japanese families worked hard to rebuild their small businesses.

For a long time Japan was quite closed to Western influences. That gradually changed and young people especially adopted many aspects of European and American fashion and culture.

Post-War Japan
During the Second World War, Japan occupied large parts of Southeast Asia. After the war, it basically lost all lands gained in the 20th century, including all territory on the mainland of Asia. Japan was reduced to its four large main islands and small offshore islands.

TERRITORIAL LOSSES

USSR
ALASKA
CHINA
MANCHURIA
JAPAN
NEW GUINEA

■ Allies
□ Territory lost by Japan to the Allies prior to August 1945
■ Japanese territory in August 1945

Civil Unrest
Many Japanese people opposed the US-Japan Security Treaty of 1952, which allowed continued American use of bases in Japan and possible intervention in disturbances within the country. A new treaty was signed in 1960, giving Japan more say in its own affairs and committing the US to defend Japan in case of attack. Some Japanese political activists still opposed any form of military alliance with the US.

Learning from the West
By the mid-1950s, Japanese industry was recovering well. Japanese businessmen and engineers studied Western industrial methods and then applied them in the new, modernized factories that had replaced old-fashioned workshops. This led the way by the 1970s to the development and mass production of high-tech electronic equipment, such as hi-fi products and computers. Japanese goods soon gained a reputation for high standards and affordable prices.

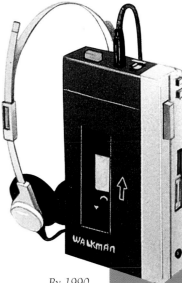

The pioneering Walkman first went on sale in Japan in 1979. It was soon a huge hit around the world.

By 1990, advertising like this was common on the high-rise buildings of Tokyo and other Japanese cities.

Booming Economy
The Japanese economy continued to grow at an enormous rate. It weathered the problems caused by sharply rising oil prices in the 1970s. Exports continued to increase as Japanese steel, cars, television sets, and other electronic products proved lastingly popular. Japan became a model for the developing nations of Southeast Asia. By the late 1980s, however, rising prices caused Japanese exports to slide from their high position.

JAPAN ON THE RISE

1946
The Allied occupation force draws up a new Japanese constitution.

1951
The Treaty of Peace with Japan is formally signed.

1954
Japan introduces the world's first transistor radio.

1955
The Liberal Democratic Party (LDP) comes to power and dominates for the rest of the period.

1956
The first Japanese car is sold in the USA.

1964
The Shinkansen (bullet train) is launched.

1975
Japan joins France, Italy, UK, USA and West Germany in the G6 forum of industrialized nations.

1982
Sony launches the compact disc (CD).

1989
Emperor Hirohito dies and is succeeded by his son Akihito. Japan joins the Asia-Pacific Economic Cooperation (APEC).

Scientific Developments

Scientists made great strides in many different fields. In medicine, new vaccines were discovered, tissue transplants were introduced, and pioneering techniques opened up the field of genetics. Scientists also learned more about ways in which human uses of chemicals and fuels were affecting the environment. Despite all these advances, however, environmental pollution increased and millions of people around the world remained without enough food or medical care.

Organ Transplants

South African surgeon Christiaan Barnard (1922–2001) performed the world's first heart transplant in 1967. For some years transplants were difficult, because patients' bodies rejected foreign tissue. In the 1980s, drugs were developed to help this problem. By 1981 the first heart-lung transplant had been performed, and four years later a heart-lung-liver transplant was completed. As techniques improved, the biggest drawback was a lack of organ donors.

The first artificial heart was implanted by American surgeon William DeVries in 1982. It was made of plastic and aluminim.

Genetics

In 1953, UK biologists Francis Crick and James Watson discovered the molecular structure of deoxyribonucleic acid (DNA), the substance that passes genetic information from one generation to the next. This was an extremely important breakthrough in understanding inherited diseases, earning the scientists a Nobel Prize. Twenty years later, researchers were able to insert genes from one species into the cells of another, leading to new techniques in genetic engineering.

Crick and Watson built a model of the structure of DNA, which looks like a twisted ladder and is called a double helix.

Vaccines

Vaccines help people by causing the body to produce antibodies against disease. In the 1950s, important vaccines became available. A vaccine against poliomyelitis was developed by the American researcher Jonas E. Salk and became available in 1955. This was followed eight years later by the first measles vaccine. A smallpox vaccination program was so successful that the disease had been wiped out by 1980.

A baby is given a vaccine by mouth in 1961. Many other vaccines are injected.

This chimp is peeling the bark off a twig to make a tool for extracting termites.

Animal Behavior

British scientist Jane Goodall made great advances in ethology—the study of animal behavior. From 1960 she studied chimpanzees in a national park in Tanzania. She found that chimpanzees were not exclusively vegetarian, as previously thought, and used tools.

Environmental Concern

New scientific discoveries about the damaging effects of environmental pollution were made throughout the period. People became concerned about nuclear waste and other hazardous substances, as well as about harm to the atmosphere's protective ozone layer caused by chlorofluorocarbons (CFCs). Protest groups sprang up, and the international organization Greenpeace was founded in 1969. Among the practical successes for environmentalists was the banning of CFC aerosols in 1978.

People joined this protest demonstration to point out the harmful dangers of car exhaust gases.

Test-tube Babies

Medical scientists developed a technique to help infertile couples have babies. Called in vitro fertilization, the technique brings male sperm and female eggs together in a laboratory. A fertilized egg is then implanted in the mother and develops as a normal baby. The first so-called test-tube baby was born in 1978. This and similar medical techniques led to debates about whether they were ethical.

A woman gives birth to test-tube twins in 1982.

Information Technology (IT)

There was a revolution in IT, as computers became smaller (see page 32). Data storage moved from magnetic tape to tape cassettes, then to floppy discs (in 1971) and compact discs (CDs). Storage was especially important, because early personal computers did not have powerful internal memories. The increased use of word processing and database operation changed the way in which many people worked.

The CD was introduced in 1982, but recordable versions were not available until 1990.

SCIENTIFIC DEVELOPMENTS

1947
American chemist Willard Frank Libby (1908–80) discovers carbon-14 and a new method of dating ancient objects.

1953
British biochemist Frederick Sanger determines the structure of a protein (insulin) for the first time.

1960
American physicist Theodore Maiman (1927–2007) builds the first laser.

1967
The World Health Organization starts a vaccination program to get rid of smallpox.

1973
A calf is produced from a frozen embryo for the first time.

1981
Solar One, the world's largest solar-power generating station goes into operation in the USA.

1990
First commercial supply of dial-up access to the Internet.

Glossary

Ballistic missile Long-range, rocket-powered missile carrying a nuclear warhead. It can fly through space, outside the Earth's atmosphere.

Brinkmanship A brink is the edge of a cliff. Leaders who practise brinkmanship take their nations to the very edge of war; if they are lucky, their opponent gives way at the last minute.

Boycott To boycott someone is to have nothing further to do with him or her; if a meeting is boycotted, nobody attends it. The word comes from a Captain Boycott in 19th-century Ireland. His tenants refused to work for him after he threw them out of their homes for not paying the rent.

Chlorofluorocarbons (CFCs) Colorless gases widely used to cool refrigerators since the 1930s, and also to propel out liquids in aerosol sprays. Because of their damaging effect on the ozone layer, their use is forbidden in many countries.

Collectivization In Communist countries, the taking over of privately owned farms by the state. Many of these were then merged together into one larger unit.

Communist bloc A term describing the Soviet Union plus its allies, the Communist-led countries of Eastern Europe.

Coup The sudden overthrow of a country's government, especially by its army officers.

Détente In French, "relaxation:" the easing of tense relationships, especially between states. It usually refers to the 1970s 'thaw' in the Cold War.

Donor Someone who gives something. Particularly refers to people who agree to let their organs be used for transplant surgery.

Gang of Four Four Chinese leaders, including Mao's widow Jiang Qing, who tried and failed to seize power after Mao's death. They were blamed for encouraging the brutal acts that took place during the Cultural Revolution.

Genes The factors that control how characteristics—height, hair color, musical ability, for example—pass from parents to children. The study of genes is called genetics. The genetic make-up of a living organism can be altered by manipulating its DNA—the new science of genetic engineering.

Glasnost In Russian, "openness." A keyword used by Soviet leader Mikhail Gorbachev in his drive during the late 1980s to make the Soviet system more efficient—and more Western in style. His policy resulted in more contact between Soviet and Western peoples, but was not popular in the USSR.

Espionage Spying on one country while working for the intelligence service of another.

Hippies A movement of young people that began in the late 1960s in California. They sought a life of freedom, peace and pleasure. Many took drugs. The name came from the low-waisted 'hipster' trousers that many of them wore.

Indian National Congress The main political party in India. Before 1947 it led the campaign for independence from British rule.

In vitro fertilization A technique for helping infertile couples to conceive, where egg and sperm are brought together in a laboratory.

Khmer Rouge A Communist movement formed in 1970 in Cambodia, which it renamed Kampuchea, and led by Pol Pot.

Lunar module The portion of the Apollo 11 rocket that actually landed on the surface of the Moon. The astronauts took off in the upper part of it to return to the 'command module' waiting in orbit, in which they returned to Earth.

Mantra A word or phrase thought to be holy and repeated over and over as a prayer or aid to meditation.

Nationalization The takeover by the state of an industry previously run by its owners or managers for its shareholders, who had each received a share of the profits.

NATO The North Atlantic Treaty Organization, an alliance of European states and the US, formed in 1949 for defense against possible Soviet aggression.

New Look Fashion launched in 1947 by designer Christian Dior. Its lavish use of fabric was welcomed with joy by women all over Europe after wartime austerities, but was criticized by governments.

Perestroika In Russian, "restructuring"—the title of a book (1987) by Soviet leader Mikhail Gorbachev. In it he explains his wish to introduce liberal ideas, reduce corruption and increase efficiency in the USSR. Popular in the West, this policy led to considerable unrest in the Soviet Union.

Plutonium A chemical element (Pu) produced in nuclear reactors that can give off immense energy if exploded.

Proletarian An expression from Marxist Communism, meaning people who work with their hands and do not own or manage businesses.

Satellite An artificial satellite is an unmanned spacecraft orbiting the Earth in space. Hundreds are currently in orbit. Their uses include weather forecasting, navigational aids to shipping and telecommunications.

Segregated "Kept apart"—a term used for the official separation of people according to their race or skin color, so that by law they must go to different schools, live in different areas, etc. This happened in South Africa under apartheid and in the southern USA.

Space Shuttle A spacecraft designed to carry people and cargo into orbit around the Earth, land and be used again.

"Star Wars" The nickname of a program intended to produce an anti-ballistic missile space defense system for the USA. Begun by President Reagan in 1983, its official name was the Strategic Defense Initiative. It was scaled down in 1991.

Un-American Activities Committee A US government committee chaired by Senator Joseph McCarthy. From 1950 to 1954 (when McCarthy was discredited) it publicly interrogated prominent people suspected of being, or of once having been, Communists.

UN charter The document agreed by the major world powers in 1945 that set out how the United Nations Organization (the UN) should operate.

USSR The Union of Soviet Socialist Republics—15 republics in eastern Europe and northern Asia, of which Russia was by far the largest. The USSR was created as a Communist state after the revolution of 1917. It was finally dissolved in 1991.

Walkman The first truly portable way to listen to music, the original (1979) Walkman was a small tape-cassette player that ran on batteries and could be listened to through headphones.

West Bank Land on the west bank of the River Jordan, formerly in the state of Jordan but captured by Israel in 1967. Most people living there are Palestinian Arabs.

Women's Lib Short for "women's liberation," a forerunner of feminism. Arising in the late 1960s, it rejected the dominance of men in the workplace and the home, and demanded improvement of women's place in society. It was particularly influential in the USA.

Zionists Campaigners since 1897 for a Jewish homeland in Palestine that would occupy all the territory believed by Jews to be 'the land of Israel' mentioned in their Scriptures.

Index